OPENING TO THE LIGHT

Opening to the Light

Weekly Meditations on Messages from Near-Death Experiences

Gary D. Guthrie

Plowshare Media
LA JOLLA, CALIFORNIA

Library of Congress Control Number: 2009936133
Guthrie, Gary D.
Opening to the Light

ISBN: 978-0-9821145-7-5 (First American paperback edition)

Cover photograph © Jon Sullivan; *Lotus Flower*, 2003; http://pdphoto.org
Interior photographs are from the public domain. Their copyrights
remain with the original holders.

Published by:
Plowshare Media
P.O. Box 278
La Jolla, CA 92038

PUBLISHER'S NOTE

Dedicated to seekers of the Light everywhere

No prayer goes unanswered

Contents

INTRODUCTION

Near-death experiences have been with humanity since time immemorial. Only since 1976 have they become known widely, following the publication of Dr. Raymond Moody's book, *Life after Life*.

Despite the vastly diverse backgrounds of near-death experiencers, their messages hold common themes. The significance of their messages is that they come directly from the source of life and offer helpful insights, which can be applied to your life here and now.

Each message is written in the form of a meditation, which includes an affirmation. Fifty-two messages were chosen to correlate with the number of weeks in a year. They are designed to inspire you in a manner similar to the way they illuminated the lives of those who originally received them.

Using this book for reflection and meditation can have a profound effect on your life. For near-death experiencers, it will reinforce your time in the Light. For non-experiencers, it can assist in making these messages part of your daily life.

In time, we become what we love and what inspires us.

Suggested Meditation Dates

Opening to the Light

In a sermon, Buddha simply held up a flower and didn't say a word. Flowers freely open to the Light.

Jesus said, "Solomon, in all his glory, was not arrayed as one of these [lilies of the field]." The truth is—we *can* open to the Light.

People who have had near-death experiences have learned that we can all open to the Light, because each of us is part of the Light. Meditation allows us a chance to experience the Light, and an extraordinary life.

During your meditation, sense
a strong desire to open to the Light.

Affirmation:

I AM CONNECTED TO AN INFINITE SOURCE

BRIGHT AND BEAUTIFUL

When you open to the Light, it is "bright and beautiful," according to near-death experiencers, and it is also "peaceful, healing, loving, and transforming."

Psychologists sometimes speak of an "inner-self-helper" that exists in each of us, which is "wise, stable, and self-organizing." This helper is similar to the Light, in that it desires our well-being and happiness.

In meditation, the Light and our inner-self-helper operate together and can change our unhealthy living patterns into higher levels of thinking and being.

During your meditation, sense that your soul (inner-self) is composed of, and aligned with, the Light.

Affirmation:

I TRUST THE GUIDANCE OF MY INNER LIGHT

DARKNESS AND THE LIGHT

A common message from the near-death experience is that "the Light is aware and within us all," despite the fact that most people live and act as if they are in darkness and alone.

An opening line of a Hindu prayer pleads, "Oh Lord, from darkness, lead me into the Light." The Koran states: "Bring forth your people from utter darkness into light …."

These are simple requests that our awareness of the Light may increase, and that there may be less greed, selfishness, and ignorance in our lives, which keep us in the dark.

During your meditation, sense your prayer for a closer relationship with the Light being answered.

Affirmation:

FROM GREED AND IGNORANCE, I AM MOVING INTO THE LIGHT

The Secret of the Ages

One significant message many near-death experiencers receive is that the Light is our home and our source. Names like "father," "mother," and "divine redeemer" are often given to the Light.

People as diverse as the Roman slave Epictetus and Paul of Tarsus wrote that the Divine lives in us as our true nature. The knowledge of this is the secret of the ages.

The key is that you *know* your inner divinity, which will lead to extraordinary events in your life.

During your meditation, sense that
you are part of a divine heritage.

Affirmation:

I KNOW THE SOURCE OF MY BEING

WEEK 5

AN ENLIGHTENED LIFE

A Tibetan-Buddhist mantra may have been inspired by ancient accounts of near-death experiences. The mantra, *om mani padme hung*, translates to:

"The jewel [a good life] is in the lotus [enlightenment]."

The lotus invites you to quiet your mind in meditation and practice a peaceful life when you're not meditating. The Dalai Lama teaches:

"Peace, love, and compassion do not just fall out of the sky—they have to be lived."

During your meditation, sense that
practicing loving actions is "enlightenment."

Affirmation:

I CAN LIVE AN ENLIGHTENED LIFE

9

A Deep Connection

In his near-death experience, John Migliaccio felt connected to everything and everyone on earth. He wanted to embrace the earth and all life upon it. He said:

"True spirituality is feeling that everything is divine and connected. It transcends religion, which often divides people into special groups."

The best religion, he learned, is "whatever brings you closer to the Light." We all belong to one undivided family proceeding from one unifying source.

During your meditation, sense yourself connected with everyone and everything.

Affirmation:

I FEEL A DEEP CONNECTION WITH ALL LIFE

WEEK 7

As a Deer in the Desert

Near-death and enlightened meditation experiencers say that, "To experience the Light is to go on seeking after the Light." This observation is also expressed in *Psalm 42*.

"As the deer longs for flowing mountain streams, so my soul longs for Thee, my Lord."

Once someone experiences the Light, they long to return. The Light is like refreshing water to the thirsty soul. When it has been tasted, one yearns for more.

*During your meditation, visualize the Light
reflecting on a cool mountain stream
from which you sip and are refreshed.*

Affirmation:

I AM REFRESHED IN THE LIGHT

LOVE EXISTS FOREVER

Yolaine Stout sensed that the Light she encountered in her near-death experience is the energy source of all life, and contains qualities of love, joy, and compassion. She said:

"Love is not something you seek; love seeks and finds you. It is the fabric of the universe; everything is full of Light."

If "everything is full of Light," it follows that each of us has the Light within our core. Bringing forth this love from within us is both our challenge and purpose in life.

During your meditation, sense that practicing love
is, and will be, the fulfillment of your life.

Affirmation:

THE LOVE AND LIGHT IN ME LIVE FOREVER

WEEK 9

AS AN OCEAN WAVE

When we perform any act of kindness in life, it places us together with all others who perform similar acts. A frequent message from near-death experiencers is that:

"The only thing we take with us after death is the love we have given away."

Giving love to others through kindness comes naturally when you realize you are a piece of the Light, just as a fractal in mathematics is composed of smaller patterns which mirror the whole.

As an ocean wave is part of the greater ocean, so are you, at your core, a part of the Light.

*During your meditation, sense yourself
as a part of a larger whole.*

Affirmation:

I AM RENEWING MY ENERGIES IN THE LIGHT

A PRECIOUS GIFT

People who had low self-esteem before having a near-death experience often say afterwards, "If the Light has that much love for me, then I must be essentially okay." A near-death experiencer, David Bennett, said:

"I experienced a love and acceptance in the Light like I had never felt before."

Lives are changed by both the experience of the Light and by coming in contact with its message. These changes include feeling, as many experiencers express, that:

"Life is a very precious gift."

During your meditation, sense the love that is in the Light.

Affirmation:

I SENSE A PRECIOUSNESS ABOUT LIFE

DURING LIFE'S STORMS

Ann Horn from Seattle, Washington said:

"My near-death experience taught me that we all have Light and Love in us sufficient to lift the fog and veils of fear around us."

Mahatma Gandhi, who faced many challenges, said: "Each of us has to find our own peace from within. And peace, to be real, must be unaffected by outside conditions."

Concentrating on the Light when facing a problem is the key to overcoming the obstacles that confront us in life.

During your meditation, sense
the Light that is within you.

Affirmation:

THROUGH ALL LIFE'S EXPERIENCES,
I STAND SERENE

The Way of the Light

Lao Tzu, a contemporary of Confucius, wrote a Chinese scripture called the *Tao Te Ching*, meaning, "The Way of the Light and Its Power."

In this classical work, he suggests that during meditation:

"Still your mind and go to an awareness of the power within the Light, become one with it, absorbing its love and power."

Chinese near-death experiencers often state that reflecting on the Light in their meditation produces results that are "peaceful and powerful."

*During your meditation, sense
the power of the Light within you.*

Affirmation:

**I SENSE THE LIGHT AND
ABSORB ITS POWER AND LOVE**

A Fear of Brilliance

Nelson Mandela said, "Our greatest fear is our brilliance." A message often received by near-death experiencers is to overcome this fear, for there is no worry, stress, or tension in the Light.

Modern physicists, such as David Bohm, state that we are enfolded in another dimension. Near-death experiencer Betty Eadie calls it being "embraced by the Light."

During times of meditation, we can ground ourselves in an awareness that we are loved and protected by the Light.

During your meditation, sense being
embraced or surrounded by the Light.

Affirmation:

I AM ENFOLDED BY AN UNSEEN POWER

ACTS OF KINDNESS

Love that we give away to others, ironically, is one of the few things that we take with us at death. Near-death experiencers often report seeing their whole life flash before them in review. Dannion Brinkley said:

"In my life review, I saw that random acts of kindness were the most important aspects of my life."

He said that these acts speak volumes about us. We will actually become, in our life reviews, the people we meet during our lifetime, and experience the effects of our actions.

One act of kindness is greater than a thousand prayers.

*During your meditation, sense
kindness and joy within you.*

Affirmation:

I AM PART OF EVERYONE I ENCOUNTER

IN A COCOON

A message that author Sandra Rogers, received from the Light was:

"Look upon the physical body as a cocoon that helps in the development of your True Self."

Our true self is our higher nature, which some people call "the soul."

The arduous change a caterpillar makes to become a butterfly is analogous to our own soul's development in becoming a being of Light.

During your meditation, sense that you are gradually changing your lower ego-nature to reflect the inner Light.

Affirmation:

I AM, INDEED, OPENING TO THE LIGHT

AN IMPRISONED SPLENDOR

A near-death experiencer, Mildred Norman Ryder, who called herself "Peace Pilgrim," taught:

"Within you is the Light of the world—share it with the world."

By sharing the Light with others, our souls work with the Divine and make the world a better place for everyone.

According to the poet Robert Browning, some near-death experiencers, and some enlightened meditators, the Light within you is "an imprisoned splendor."

During your meditation, sense the Light within you and your ability to share it with others.

Affirmation:

I SENSE BOTH LIGHT AND LOVE WITHIN MYSELF

A MATRIX OF SOULS

In his near-death experience, Mellen-Thomas Benedict witnessed the 'imprisoned splendor' and was told how to increase his spiritual development:

"Begin by loving the inner Light in yourself, and then you will love everything and everyone out of that."

He also learned that "we are all connected, composing a greater being, a matrix of human souls; whatever we do to others affects the whole matrix."

The matrix, he said, was like being enveloped in an enormous, close-knit, loving family.

During your meditation, sense a splendorous
Light within yourself and others.

Affirmation:

I CHERISH THE LIGHT IN EVERY FORM

This Present Moment

Both near-death and enlightened meditation experiencers sometimes find themselves stopping to cherish the present moment, and shedding tears of joy for the sheer, miraculous, beauty of life. Their message is:

"Cherish the moment you are in with gratitude and joy."

Each today and tomorrow is one precious moment, a special gift from the Light.

A suggestion in many meditation practices is to feel that you are one with "Beingness" (life-energy/God).

*During your meditation, feel totally
at one with the present moment.*

Affirmation:

I AM FULLY AWARE OF THIS PRESENT MOMENT

AN INEFFABLE BEAUTY

"Ineffable" and "beautiful" are words that are often used to describe the Light and the other side of life that eventually await us.

Siddhartha Gautama, known as "Buddha," said the Light was indescribable, yet offered a few adjectives:

" … deathless, peaceful, blissful, radiant, changeless Nirvana."

In Christianity, both the Light and the other side of life are called "the peace that passes understanding."

During your meditation, sense that you are
part of this peace, and feel it's beauty and bliss.

Affirmation:

I AM FILLED WITH PEACE WITHIN

Empowered by the Light

Arthur Yensen had a near-death experience in a car accident, and twenty years later, in 1955, wrote a pamphlet entitled: *I Saw Heaven and It Changed My Life.*

He said that the knowledge that there is a wonderful life waiting for us sustained him through many difficulties and hardships. He wrote that he was "empowered by the Light."

P.M.H. Atwater, quoting Frank Herbert, the author of *Dune*, wrote of her empowerment from the Light:

"I will face my fears, go through them, and I shall remain."

During your meditation, sense yourself empowered from the source of life.

Affirmation:

I AM EMPOWERED BY THE LIGHT

AS IF IT WERE MY OWN LIFE

Dr. Melvin Morse wrote, "A patient, twenty years after seeing the Light, told me:

'I will never forget that Light—it is always with me, as if it were my own life.'"

This is essentially my own experience. Along with other experiencers, I feel that in times of difficulties, if we remember the love in the Light and consult with it, things get better.

Embedded somewhere in every soul is a memory of the Light that can be rekindled.

During your meditation, sense yourself
being totally open to the love within the Light.

Affirmation:

I AM OPENING TO THE LOVING LIGHT

AN INCREDIBLE VALUE

Dr. Kenneth Ring described one college student who sensed during his near-death experience that his soul was like "a ball of Light, bathed in total love and radiance."

The experience changed his life completely. He no longer desired expensive physical objects, but cherished what he called "an incredible value"—things like sunsets, trees, animals, and friends.

He began following his inner Light to cooperate with others rather than being highly competitive, as he had been before his experience.

During your meditation, sense your own soul
filled with the love and radiance of the Light.

Affirmation:

I AM ONE WITH THE LIGHT

GROWING TO HEAVEN

Near-death experiencers often describe themselves having felt like "a ball of Light-energy," raised to a location they depict as a "paradise" or "heaven."

Edgar Cayce observed: "You grow to heaven, you don't go to heaven." The word "heaven" in Aramaic, he pointed out, is interchangeable with the word "leaven."

He further observed that the qualities of love, joy, and peace increase within us as we progress. Trusting both the Light and the process during our meditation assists in "leavening the soul."

During your meditation, sense the Light assisting the growth of love, joy, and peace within you.

Affirmation:

I SENSE THE LIGHT INCREASING WITHIN ME

EMBRACED BY THE INFINITE

The greatest love any of us will ever experience is the love between our soul and the Light. It is a union in which we are embraced by the infinite, and yet we do not always sense this embrace.

This is why some spiritual people and mystics "court" the Divine as a lover or beloved. Robert Browning wrote a verse mystics sometimes quote in which the Light speaks to each of us individually:

"Come, grow old along with me. The best is yet to be! A Whole I made .... Trust me. See all! Be not afraid."

During your meditation, sense yourself
filled and embraced by the Light.

Affirmation:

I TRUST THEE COMPLETELY, BELOVED LIGHT

WHAT WE TAKE WITH US

Several near-death experiencers have received this message in the Light:

"Love and knowledge are the only two things you bring with you after this life."

Every material possession you have, you will leave behind. The only thing that you will take with you is the inner Light, to whatever degree it is developed. A near-death experiencer, Sandra Rogers, said:

"We take with us what we are, not what we own."

During your meditation, visualize yourself growing in love and knowledge.

Affirmation:

I CHERISH LOVE AND KNOWLEDGE

FORGIVENESS AND ECSTASY

Forgiveness can lead us to ecstasy, yet many of us refuse to absolve others and often find it even more difficult to forgive our own shortcomings.

Part of love includes total forgiveness. There is a saying among seekers of truth: "to die before you die." It means to surrender ego and let go of hurts, resentments, and other negative feelings.

An infinite ecstasy comes from forgiveness. A function of meditation, and of our inner-self-helper, is to assist us in forgiving ourselves and others.

During your meditation, sense
your higher self helping you to forgive.

Affirmation:

I FORGIVE EVERYONE AND EVERYTHING

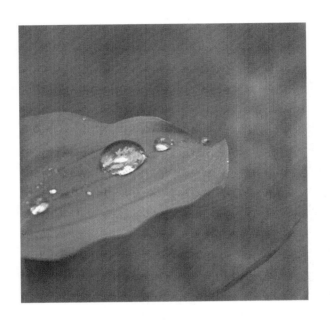

OUR GREATEST JOY

The ancient Egyptians believed that they would be asked two questions during their life review: "Did you bring joy?" and "Did you find joy?"

It is easier to find joy when your wants and needs are simple, and easier to give joy when you are genuinely open and sincere with others.

Near-death experiencers state that their greatest joy came through experiencing love directly from the Light. They also say that to share this love with others brings immense joy.

During your meditation, see yourself
both receiving and sharing joy with others.

Affirmation:

I BOTH BRING AND FIND JOY

REFRESHED BY LOVING LIGHT

Light is at the center of the near-death experience. This loving life-essence lives in each of us, as it lives everywhere else. Light is everywhere and within everything.

Mellen-Thomas Benedict learned through his near-death experience that "we save, redeem, and heal ourselves; we always have, we always will."

Meditation often refreshes us by reducing tensions and fears. Offering up our mistakes to be forgiven and healed in the Light can help us leave them behind.

*During your meditation, sense yourself
receiving forgiveness directly from the Light.*

Affirmation:

I AM AT PEACE IN THE LIGHT

Courage in Adversity

Dr. Kenneth Ring described a terribly abused, seven-year-old girl who, in a suicide attempt, was told in the Light, "although nobody cares about you, it is your job to care about yourself."

She was shown a barren winter tree and the same tree filled with leaves in the summer, demonstrating to her that there are seeds of hope in every adversity.

Surviving life's tragedies takes great courage. A common message that near-death experiencers receive is:

"Everything that happens in life occurs for a particular reason. In time, all things will be made clear."

During your meditation, sense yourself caring deeply about your own well-being, along with that of others.

Affirmation:

I LOVE AND CARE ABOUT MYSELF AND OTHERS

AFTER ENLIGHTENMENT

One of the most difficult tasks facing some meditators and near-death experiencers is coming back to the physical world after experiencing the Light in any form.

A famous Zen Buddhist saying is:

"Before enlightenment, I chopped wood and carried water. After enlightenment, I chop wood and carry water."

After enlightenment, the river of life remains the same, but one gains an enhanced awareness to forge the tumbling waters as they flow downstream.

During your meditation, sense an awareness of the Light.

Affirmation:

I AM AWARE OF A LIVING PRESENCE

COURTING THE DIVINE

A famous mystic, Jan van Ruysbroeck, said that our relationship to the Divine in meditation is like "a lover and a beloved." He said further:

"God, in the depth of us, receives God, who comes to us. It is God contemplating God."

One near-death experiencer, Beverly Brodsky, said, "After all these years, from the time of our near-death experiences to now, we still hunger for that love and connection we experienced in the Light."

Meditation is sometimes considered a form of nurturing, a love relationship or courtship with the Divine.

*During your meditation, sense
your love for the Divine increasing.*

Affirmation:

I LOVE THE DIVINE IN EVERY ASPECT OF MY LIFE

SEEING WITH THE HEART

Antoine de Saint-Exupéry, the author of *The Little Prince*, may have had a near-death experience in the Sahara Desert. He wrote of a small prince, who could have been a being of Light, telling him:

"It is only with the heart that one sees rightly; what is essential is invisible to the eye."

"Seeing with the heart" is the practice of using one's spiritual eyes to look behind sometimes cold and cruel worldly facades, to perceive the inner Light in others and within one's own self.

During your meditation, sense yourself growing in insight and inspiration.

Affirmation:

I SEE AND HEAR WITH SPIRITUAL SENSES

HAPPINESS

Happiness is elusive and often fleeting for many people who seek it. Near-death experiencers equate happiness with the love they find within the Light.

A Hindu Upanishad identifies happiness and joy with the Light, saying:

"From the joy of the Light all beings have come, by joy they live, and unto joy they shall return."

When we live in an awareness of the Light, the joy of our destination can be felt in the journey, here and now.

*During your meditation, sense
that happiness is your birthright.*

Affirmation:

THE JOY OF THE LIGHT IS MY STRENGTH

AT HOME IN THE UNIVERSE

Philip Berman, a near-death experiencer, learned that "The universe is a living presence, and the foundation of it is love." He said further:

> "There is real peace and comfort when you feel part of the Light and completely at home in the universe."

Dr. Melvin Morse reports that a common message among children who have near-death experiences is:

> "The Light is a Loving Presence that unifies everything in life."

During your meditation, sense yourself
unified by a loving presence.

Affirmation:

MY SOUL AND THE LIGHT ARE ONE

A UNIQUE ADVENTURE

The message that Kimberly Clark-Sharp received in the Light is that life is a unique adventure in learning to love:

"Why are we here? *To learn.*
What is the purpose of life? *To love.*"

She was also told that, with time and patience, we will eventually learn to love everyone equally and unconditionally.

She, along with many other near-death experiencers, has learned to see life as an adventure rather than an agony to be endured.

*During your meditation, sense yourself
enjoying the learning time on earth.*

Affirmation:

MY LIFE IS A UNIQUE ADVENTURE

ALL THINGS SHALL BE WELL

The English mystic, Julian of Norwich, may have also had a near-death experience. Her writings are very positive and life-affirming, resembling modern near-death experience accounts. Julian wrote:

"I learned that all things are and shall be well."

Paul of Tarsus, who had an encounter with the Light near Damascus, related a similar message, paraphrased in a letter to the Philippians:

"He [the Light] which began a good work in you, will be faithful to complete it."

During your meditation, visualize yourself
as part of a loving and intelligent power.

Affirmation:

ALL THINGS ARE AND SHALL BE WELL

WEEK 37

THE PRECIOUSNESS OF LIFE

How we respond to the events in our life is the most important aspect of our life review, according to many near-death experiencers. Dr. Melvin Morse quotes a child experiencer:

> "Nothing in life is worth getting upset over. The Light convinced me that life is very precious, and that there is much more to life than most people imagine."

In meditation, one's horizons begin to increase as one sits in silence with the Light, and the preciousness of life reveals itself.

During your meditation, sense yourself being open to an expanded view of this life and eternity.

Affirmation:

I SENSE THE BREVITY AND PRECIOUSNESS OF LIFE

NO GREATER TRUTH

George Ritchie, a near-death experiencer and psychiatrist wrote:

"We cannot see others as loveable until we see ourselves as loveable."

Light and love interwoven are the ultimate reality of life. Bonnie Burrows said:

"During my near-death experience, I learned that love is what life is all about. It is everything, and everything is love. There is no greater truth than this."

During your meditation, sense yourself as loveable, both in receiving and giving love.

Affirmation:

THERE IS NO GREATER TRUTH
IN MY LIFE THAN LOVE

ASPIRE TO LIVE JOYFULLY

Near-death experiencer Andy Petro says that the Light is like a magnet that draws us toward it, and that we can aspire to have qualities that are part of the Light. He said:

"If I want peace to live in me, I must live in peace.
If I want joy to live in me, I must be joyful."

Aspiring to live meaningfully and joyfully was a goal of the ancient Greeks, who carved on their temple the words *gnothi seauton*, meaning "know thyself."

Know yourself as a child of the Light.

*During your meditation, sense
that joy is innately within you.*

Affirmation:

I AWAKEN EACH DAY TO THE JOY WITHIN ME

RESPONDING LIKE A TREE

Psalm 1 compares each of us to a tree. A tree is rooted in the earth, bends with the wind, and responds to the sun. A wise person is grounded in the source of life, resilient to life's storms, and aware of the presence of the Light.

The awareness of Light often comes with a change in attitude. Marcel Proust wrote:

"The path to wisdom is not in seeing new vistas, but in having new eyes."

While on a river in Africa, Dr. Albert Schweitzer's inner spiritual senses were awakened. His "new eyes" showed him that nature and animals emit a silent and unconditional love.

During your meditation, sense
the Divine living within all nature and life.

Affirmation:

I AM WISE AND GROUNDED IN
THE PRESENCE OF THE LIGHT

WEEK 41

AN AGELESS HIGHER SELF

Sandra Rogers was told in the Light that "Your true self is timeless, ageless, and tireless."

Common sense tells us that while we are wearing a physical body, we will feel better by eating healthier, thinking positive thoughts, and by eliminating fear and stress from our lives.

Mildred Norman Ryder added:

"To have a constant awareness of God's presence is to feel peace within—a calm, serene confidence, which enables you to face any situation in life."

During your meditation, sense the presence of the Light—its serenity and confidence.

Affirmation:

I AM AWARE OF THE LIGHT WITHIN ME

Loved by the Light

After years of near-death experience research, Dr. Melvin Morse wrote:

"We should feel excited that the Light is ever present in our life, and that It loves us beyond our wildest comprehension."

Our interactions with the other side of life will be as with members of a close-knit family. He said further:

"As we revere life, it is possible to interact with the Light and Beings of Light, here and now."

*During your meditation, sense
an interaction with the Light.*

Affirmation:

MY LIFE IS AN INTERACTION WITH THE LIGHT

THE GLOW OF CANDLELIGHT

The Light that near-death experiencers encounter is often described as a "bright, white light that does not burn the eyes," or "like the glow of candlelight," with the feeling of love, warmth, and "being at home in the Light."

The Spanish mystic, St. John of the Cross, wrote concerning the Light in nature and meditation:

> "My beloved is the mountains
>   and lonely wooded valleys...
> Strange islands and resounding rivers...
>   Silent Music, sounding solitude...
> The supper that refreshes and deepens love."

*During your meditation, sense yourself
at home in the Light.*

Affirmation:

I AM ONE WITH THE SOURCE OF LIFE

LIFE-TRANSFORMING EXPERIENCES

Without being near-death or in enlightened meditation, Bede Griffiths had a spiritually transforming experience that completely changed his life.

As a seminary student, he responded to a passage from *Psalm 13*:3, "Lord, enlighten my eyes," with a prayer: "Open my eyes that I may see wondrous things."

He said that as he walked outside, his inner spiritual senses were awakened in such a way that:

"The hard casing of exterior reality seemed to open, and everything disclosed its Inner Light."

During your meditation, visualize
all things energized by Light.

Affirmation:

I AM OPENING MY EYES THAT I
MAY SEE WONDROUS THINGS

The Beloved Light

During his times of meditation and prayer, Jesus called the Light "abba," an Aramaic word meaning both "beloved" and "father." He stated several times, "The Father and I are one."

He also taught that "the Kingdom" is an alternative reality right here in our presence—under our very noses, if we could only see it.

Many Christian near-death experiencers meet Jesus as their guide in the Light, and receive the message that we are all one and loved intensely. When internalized, this knowledge of God's love becomes a "pearl of great price."

During your meditation, sense the
feeling of being as one with the Light.

Affirmation:

THE BELOVED LIGHT AND I ARE ONE

AN INFINITE DANCE OF LIFE

The Light is within galaxies as energy—recycling itself in an infinite dance of life and death and life, endlessly.

Poets such as Walt Whitman, William Blake, William Wordsworth, Robert Browning, and the Sufi poet, Rumi, sensed the Divine within life.

Whitman saw the Divine in "a blade of grass," Blake in "a grain of sand." Wordsworth felt "a presence of joy," and Browning sensed "an imprisoned Splendor." Modern poet and near-death experiencer, Mellen-Thomas Benedict, wrote:

"You and I are God exploring Itself in an infinite dance of Light and life."

*During your meditation, visualize
your life as an infinite dance of Light.*

Affirmation:

I AM DANCING IN THE LIGHT

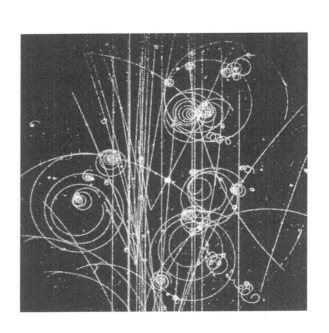

Week 47

SENSING LOVE'S PRESENCE

Although life is a dance of Light and energy, like a beautiful symphony, many people suffer from moments of sheer monotony, boredom, and depression.

Near-death experiencers have had their self-esteem raised by the messages of love they received in the Light. They speak of its healing love. Yolaine Stout was told by a being of Light:

"Do not waste your life thinking you are not loved
—for that is definitely not the case."

The acceptance she felt from the loving Light was wonderful. She said, "It literally transcended anything that words can describe."

During your meditation, sense a
loving presence around and within you.

Affirmation:

I FEEL THE LOVING LIGHT AROUND ME

GRATITUDE FOR LIFE

Mellen-Thomas Benedict received the message in the Light that, as pieces of the Divine, we inherit the ability to love unconditionally. He said:

"Because we are so greatly loved by the Light, we should love our own life in response."

The medieval mystic, Meister Eckhardt, wrote:

"If the only prayer you say in your life is 'Thank you,' that will suffice."

During this meditation,
sense a love for your own life.

Affirmation:

THANK YOU, GOD, FOR MY LIFE

BRINGING JOY TO THE WORLD

George Rodonaia was a Soviet atheist who, after a near-death experience, wrote about the message he received in the Light:

"If we simply love nature, people, animals, and creation itself, we bring joy to ourselves and others."

In gratitude, George wanted to give something back to others to help bring joy to the world. He said that for him:

"… the only meaningful life is to serve God's creation with warm and loving generosity and compassion."

During your meditation, see yourself loving nature, people, animals, and creation.

Affirmation:

I LOVE ALL NATURE AND LIFE

BEING FILLED WITH LIGHT

Perhaps the most oft-repeated message given to many near-death experiencers is:

"Love is all there is, and love is all that matters."

We have a greater chance to be filled with an awareness of the Light by avoiding greed, lies, and selfishness; and instead, developing genuine love through our meditation.

George Rodonaia learned from the Light:

"When you radiate goodwill and empathy, you open yourself to receive the fullness of God's Love."

During your meditation, sense that
genuine love is growing within you.

Affirmation:

I AM OPEN TO EXPERIENCE AND
EMIT MORE LIGHT AND LOVE

AWARENESS OF THE LIGHT

A famous Hindu phrase, *Sat-Chit-Ananda,* translates to "the awareness of the Light is bliss." It means that we can recover an awareness we had of the Light before being born.

Messages from near-death experiencers have a similar theme—that we don't have to wait until we arrive back into the Light to recover this awareness.

Anytime during our life on earth, we can seek an awareness of the Light, and it will help us, particularly during stressful times.

During your meditation, sense
an awareness of the Light within you.

Affirmation:

MY AWARENESS OF THE LIGHT IS BLISS

Act as if You Were Aware

A Jewish rabbi, Aaron of Karlin, said:

"Act as if the radiant Light of God were fully conscious in your life now."

When attempting to be the Light in action, we will be helped by hidden hands. Buckminster Fuller said:

"God is a verb, not a noun."

This is a key to achieving greater awareness of the Light. When we become the Light in our actions, peace will fill our lives and make our meditations more meaningful.

During your meditation, sense a gratitude that you have come this far on your journey in life.

Affirmation:

THE RADIANT LIGHT IS BECOMING MORE CONSCIOUS IN ME NOW

NOTES AND BIBLIOGRAPHY

Week 1. The quotation by Jesus appears in Matthew 6:29.

Week 2. Hacking, Ian, *Rewriting the Soul: Multiple Personality and the Science of Memory*, Princeton Univ. Press, N.J., 2001.

Week 3. Brihadaranyaka Upanishad 1:3.

Week 4. Colossians 1:27: "The secret of the ages is Christ within you, your hope of glory."

Week 5. Dalai Lama interview featured in the 2002 video, *Peace Pilgrim, the Sage who Walked Her Talk*.

Week 6. John Migliaccio interview featured in the 1991 video, *Round Trip*.

Week 7. Psalms 42:1-2.

Week 8. Quotation from Yolaine Stout, used by permission in private communication, 2008.

Week 10. Quotation from David Bennett: Seattle IANDS newsletter, July/Aug. 2008.

Week 11. Ann Horn interview, Seattle IANDS newsletter, Sept./Oct. 2003.

Week 12. Lao Tzu, *Tao Te Ching*, Vintage Books, N.Y., 1972.

Week 13. Nelson Mandela quote from Williamson, Marianne, *A Return to Love*, Harper Collins, N.Y., 1992.

Week 14. Brinkley, Dannion, *Saved by the Light*, Warner Books, N.Y., 1994

Week 15. Rogers, Sandra, *Lessons from the Light*, Warner Books, N.Y., 1995.

Week 16. *Peace Pilgrim, Her Life and Works in her Own Words*, Ocean Tree Press, Santa Fe, N.M., 1983, page 74.

Week 17. Benedict, Mellen-Thomas, quoted in Bailey, Lee, *The Near-Death Experience: A Reader*, Routledge, N.Y., 1996, chapter 1.

Week 18. The title for "This Present Moment" comes from Guthrie, Gary D., *A String of Pearls*, unpublished manuscript.

Week 19. Walsche, Maurice, *Buddha: Life and Word*, New Dehli, Grail Foundation Press, 1991.

Week 20. Arthur Yensen quoted in Atwater, P.M.H., *The Complete Idiot's Guide to the Near-Death Experience*, Alpha Books, Indianapolis, IN., 2000, pages 34-35.

Week 21. Morse, Dr. Melvin, *Closer to the Light*, Villard Books, N.Y., 1990, page 116.

Week 22. Ring, Ph.D., Kenneth, *Lessons from the Light*, Insight Books, N.Y., 1998, pages 11-20.

Week 23. Kirkpatrick, Sidney, *Edgar Cayce: An American Prophet*, Riverhead Books, N.Y., 2002.

Week 24. Browning, Robert, *The Poems and Plays of Robert Browning*, Modern Library, N.Y., 2002.

Week 25. Rogers, Sandra, op. cit., page 25.

Week 26. Williamson, Marianne, op. cit., page 276.

Week 27. Novak, Peter, *Journal of Near-Death Studies*, Human Sciences Press, Vol. 20, Number 3, March 2002.

Week 28. Mellen-Thomas Benedict's near-death experience featured in Bailey, Lee, op. cit., chapter 1.

Week 29. Ring, Ph.D., Kenneth, op. cit., pages 11-20.

Week 30. Johnston, William, *Silent Music: The Science of Meditation*, Harper and Row, N.Y., 1974.

Week 31. Quotation from Beverly Brodsky, used by permission in private conversation, 2008.

Week 32. Saint-Exupéry, Antoine de, *The Little Prince*, Harcourt, Brace and World, N.Y., 1943.

Week 33. Taittirya Upanishad 3:5.

Week 34. Berman, Phillip, *The Journey Home: What Near-Death Experiences Teach Us about the Gift of Life*, Simon and Schuster, N.Y., 1996, page 7.

Week 35. Sharp, Kimberly Clark, *After the Light*, Authors Choice Press, Lincoln, NE., 1995, page 26.

Week 36. Julian of Norwich, *Showing of Julian of Norwich*, W. W. Norton, London, U.K., 2004.

Week 37. Morse, Dr. Melvin, op. cit., pages 129-130.

Week 38. Ritchie, Dr. George, *My Life after Dying*, Hampton Roads Publishing Co., Norfolk, VA., 1998, pages 130-131.

Week 39. Andy Petro, quoted in Berman, Phillip, op. cit., page 125.

Week 40. Guthrie, Gary D., *The Wisdom Tree*, Ocean Tree Books, Santa Fe, NM, 1997.

Week 41. Rogers, Sandra, op. cit., page 17.
Peace Pilgrim, op. cit., page 87.

Week 42. Morse, Dr. Melvin and Perry, Paul, *Parting Visions*, Villard Books, N.Y., 1994, page 165-7.

Week 43. Verse from St. John of the Cross in Johnston, William, op. cit.

Week 44. Griffiths, Bede, and Matus, Thomas, *Bede Griffiths Essential Writings*, Orbis Books, N.Y., 2004.

Week 45. Chopra, Deepak, *The Third Jesus*, Harmony Books, N.Y., 2008.

Week 46. Mellen-Thomas Benedict quotation from Bailey, Lee, op. cit., chapter 1.

Week 47. Quotation from Yolaine Stout, used by permission in private conversation, 2008.

Week 48. Fox, Matthew, *Meditations with Meister Eckhart*, Bear and Company, Rochester, VT., 1983.

Week 49. Rodonaia, George, quoted in Bailey, Lee, op. cit., page 16.

Week 50. Rodonaia, George, quoted in Bailey, Lee, op. cit., page 16.

Week 51. *Sat-Chit-Ananda* is a Sanskrit term in Hinduism. It translates closely to the saying by Jesus: "The Kingdom of Heaven is within you." Phabhupada, A.C., *Bhagavad-Gita As It Is*, N.Y., Bhaktivedanta Book Trust, 1994.

Week 52. Aaron of Karlin, quoted in Berman, Phillip, op. cit., page 87.

Photographs

Bureau of Land Management   http://www.blm.gov

     Page 6, Nevada, *Rock Formations in the Mount Irish Wilderness Area, East of Hiko,* 2009; Page 22, Montana, *Early Monrning on the Blackfoot River,* 2008; Page 26, Oregon, *Goose Nest Near Borax Lake,* 2008; Page 34, California, *Royal Trumpter Swan*; Page 36, Alaska, *Sunset and Icebergs, Tangle Lakes*; Page 50, Wyoming, *Scenic Rock Site,* 2008.

U.S. Fish and Wildlife Service   http://www.fws.gov

     Page 12, *White-Tailed Deer Fawn,* 2004, Tom Stehn; Page 72, *Rocky Mountain Columbine,* 1980s, Dr. Thomas G. Barnes.

National Oceanic & Atmospheric Administration (NOAA)
           http://www.noaa.gov

     Page 20, *Hurricane,* 2005, image from satallite data; Page 24, *Lightning,* Orange, Australia, Shane Lear; Page 70, *Reflections,* Olympic Coast, NMS; Page 80, *San Miguel Island,* Glenn Allen; Page 82, *Kelp and Sardines,* Anacapa Island, Channel Islands National Marine Sanctuary; Page 96, *Stellar Sea Lions,* Bob Wilson.

National Aeronautics and Space Administration (NASA)
           http://www.nasa.gov

     Page 10, *Earth,* courtesy of the Image Science & Analysis Laboratory, NASA Johnson Space Center (http://eol.jsc.nasa.gov); Page 30, *Pipsqueak Star Unleashes Monster Flare,* Casey Reed/NASA; Page 40, *Total Solar Eclipse of October 24, 1995–as seen from Dundlod, India,* Fred Espenak/NASA's Goddard Space Flight Center; Page 42, *Illustration of Crystal Formation,* NASA/JPL-Caltech; Page 46, *Magnificant Details in a Dusty Spiral Galaxy,* Hubble Space Telescope Institute; Page 60, *Artist's View of Extra Solar Planet HD 189733b,* NASA/ESA/G. Bacon (STScI); Page 66, *Stephan's Quintet,* X-ray: NASA/CXC/CfA/E, O'Sullivan Optical: Canada–France–Hawaii-Telescope/Coelum; Page 68, *Ant Nebula,* NASA/ESA Hubble Space

Telescope image; Page 74, *White Dwarf, Called Sirius B*, NASA, ESA, H. Bond (STScI) and M. Barstow (University of Leicester); Page 88, *Illustration of the Milky Way*, NASA/JPL-Caltech; Page 98, *ESA and the Hubble Heritage Team (STScI/AURA)*, Casey Reed/NASA.

U.S. National Park Service   http://www.nps.gov

Page 28, *Anise Swallowtail (Papilio zelicaon)*; TKN; 1974.

Interactions.org   http://www.interactions.org

Page 92, *Bubble Chamber in 1970: Liquid Hydrogen Event* (© CERN).

Personal Public Domain Photographs from:

Thomas P. Tweed—Page xiv, *Bauhinia Blossom*, 2009; Page 48, *Dandelion Seeds*, 2009.

http://photos8.com

Page 2, The Beautiful Sky, 2009; Page 76, *Rocky Mountains, Canada*.

http://www.public-domain-photos.com

Page 44, *Wheat2*, Magnus Rosendahl; Page 56, *Magic Tree*, Paolo Neo.

http://www.publicdomainpictures.net/

Page 4, *Blue Fractal*, Tammy Pinarbas, 2008; Page 38, *Beach Uvero Alto*, 2008, Anna Cervova; Page 78, *Tree in Fog at Night*, 2009 Petr Kratochvil; Page 86, *In the Wood*, 2007, Petr Kratochvil.

http://pdphoto.org/

Jon Sullivan—Page 6, *Orderville Canyon*, 2003; Page 8, *Lotus Blossom*, 2004; Page 14, *Rose*, 2006; Page 16, *Ocean!*, 2003; Page 18, *Rays on the Meadow*, 2003; Page 32, *Dew and Spiderwebs*, 2004; Page 52, *River Rain*, 2006; Page 54, *Moraine Lake in Banff*, 2004; Page 58, *Firehole Falls at Dusk*, 2003; Page 62, *Sand Dunes*, 2003; Page 64, *Old Faithful Geyser*, 2003; Page 84, *Candle Flame*, 2005; Page 90, *Leaves*, 2009; Page 94, Zion, 2002; Page 100, *Storm Cloud*, 2009; Page 102 (and cover), *Lotus Flower*, 2003.

ACKNOWLEDGEMENTS

From the many mentors and friends who contributed to the text of this book, I wish to acknowledge Thair Milne, Dr. Melvin Morse, Ann Rush, and Beverly Brodsky for allowing their brilliance to shine forth.

From those who assisted with the photographs, I wish to acknowledge Phyllis Shamoon, as well as Shirley Ruth. Their efforts remind me of Albert Einstein's admonition to "look deeply into nature, and then you will understand everything better."

For those who approach the Light in meditation I both acknowledge and encourage your efforts. In time you will appreciate your endeavors, for that which awaits you is the splendor within.

ABOUT THE AUTHOR

Gary Guthrie had a near-death experience in 1982, when he was a college instructor overseas. Since that time, he has been active in near-death research and in meditation practice. He has lived and studied in India, the Middle East, Japan, and Singapore. Besides teaching, he has worked as a hospital chaplain and in hospice settings. He is also the author of the book, *The Wisdom Tree, a Journey to the Heart of God*, published by Ocean Tree Books, Santa Fe, New Mexico.